Sir William Berkeley

Governor of Virginia

Colonial Leaders

Lord Baltimore
English Politician and Colonist

Benjamin Banneker
American Mathematician and Astronomer

Sir William Berkeley
Governor of Virginia

William Bradford
Governor of Plymouth Colony

Jonathan Edwards
Colonial Religious Leader

Benjamin Franklin
American Statesman, Scientist, and Writer

Anne Hutchinson
Religious Leader

Cotton Mather
Author, Clergyman, and Scholar

Increase Mather
Clergyman and Scholar

James Oglethorpe
Humanitarian and Soldier

William Penn
Founder of Democracy

Sir Walter Raleigh
English Explorer and Author

Caesar Rodney
American Patriot

John Smith
English Explorer and Colonist

Miles Standish
Plymouth Colony Leader

Peter Stuyvesant
Dutch Military Leader

George Whitefield
Clergyman and Scholar

Roger Williams
Founder of Rhode Island

John Winthrop
Politician and Statesman

John Peter Zenger
Free Press Advocate

Revolutionary War Leaders

John Adams
Second U.S. President

Ethan Allen
Revolutionary Hero

Benedict Arnold
Traitor to the Cause

King George III
English Monarch

Nathanael Greene
Military Leader

Nathan Hale
Revolutionary Hero

Alexander Hamilton
First U.S. Secretary of the Treasury

John Hancock
President of the Continental Congress

Patrick Henry
American Statesman and Speaker

John Jay
First Chief Justice of the Supreme Court

Thomas Jefferson
Author of the Declaration of Independence

John Paul Jones
Father of the U.S. Navy

Lafayette
French Freedom Fighter

James Madison
Father of the Constitution

Francis Marion
The Swamp Fox

James Monroe
American Statesman

Thomas Paine
Political Writer

Paul Revere
American Patriot

Betsy Ross
American Patriot

George Washington
First U.S. President

Famous Figures of the Civil War Era

Jefferson Davis
Confederate President

Frederick Douglass
Abolitionist and Author

Ulysses S. Grant
Military Leader and President

Stonewall Jackson
Confederate General

Robert E. Lee
Confederate General

Abraham Lincoln
Civil War President

William Sherman
Union General

Harriet Beecher Stowe
Author of Uncle Tom's Cabin

Sojourner Truth
Abolitionist, Suffragist, and Preacher

Harriet Tubman
Leader of the Underground Railroad

Sir William Berkeley

Governor of Virginia

Phelan Powell

Arthur M. Schlesinger, jr.
Senior Consulting Editor

Chelsea House Publishers

Philadelphia

Produced by Pre-Press Company, Inc., East Bridgewater, MA 02333

CHELSEA HOUSE PUBLISHERS
Editor in Chief Stephen Reginald
Production Manager Pamela Loos
Art Director Sara Davis
Director of Photography Judy L. Hasday
Managing Editor James D. Gallagher
Senior Production Editor J. Christopher Higgins

Staff for *WILLIAM BERKELEY*
Project Editor Anne Hill
Associate Art Director Takeshi Takahashi
Series Design Keith Trego

The Chelsea House World Wide Web address is http://www.chelseahouse.com

First Printing
1 3 5 7 9 8 6 4 2

Library of Congress Cataloging-in-Publication Data
Powell, Phelan
    Sir William Bekeley/Phelan Powell.
       p. cm.—(colonial leaders)
    Includes bibliographical references (p.) and index.
    ISBN 0-7910-6116-7—ISBN 0-7910-6117-5 (pbk)
    1. Berkeley, William, Sir, 1608–1677—Juvenile literature. 2. Governors—
Virginia—Biography—Juvenile literature. 3. Virginia—History—Colonial
period, ca. 1660–1775—Juvenile literature. 4. Bacon's Rebellion, 1676—
Juvenile literature. [1. Berkeley, William, Sir, 1608–1677. 2. Governors.
3. Bacon's Rebellion, 1676. 4. Virgina—History—Colonial period, ca.
1600–1775.] I. Title. II. Series

F229.B53 P69 2000
975.5'020'092—dc21
[B]
                                                                00-031565

Publisher's Note: In Colonial and Revolutionary War America, there were no standard rules for spelling, punctuation, capitalization, or grammar. Some of the quotations that appear in the Colonial Leaders and Revolutionary War Leaders series come from original documents and letters written during this time in history. Original quotations reflect writing inconsistencies of the period.

Contents

As citizens of England became increasingly frustrated by the actions of King James I, they turned to the members of Parliament for help. King James, feeling threatened by the power of Parliament, had it dissolved to silence the voice of the people.

Coming of Age in the Stuart Dynasty

illiam Berkeley was born in 1606 in Bruton, England. The fortunate child was the youngest son of Sir Maurice Berkeley. The Berkeley family enjoyed the favor of King James I. James was one of the Stuarts, a noble family from Scotland. Three years earlier, he'd become the first Stuart king of England, and his descendants would rule until 1714. William's family had often been invited to the king's court, and they had much to do with issues of public importance.

England was not a very large country. Most of the citizens were poor. Only a small percentage, like

William and his family, had wealth and prestige. But William was born during a time of great change in England and the world. For centuries, the civilized people of Western Europe had accepted the rule of the Roman Catholic Church. The head of the Roman Catholic faith was the pope. Religious faith was one of the most powerful forces in the lives of the people of the early 17th century. However, more than 70 years before William was born, a major upheaval in belief in the rules of the papal church had occurred.

In the 1580s, King Henry VIII decreed that he, not the pope, was the head of the Church of England. By the time James took the throne in 1603, most people followed the Church of Enland. Some people remained Roman Catholics, but they had to practice their beliefs secretly. Others became Puritans, practicing a very strict way of living out their religion.

King James thought it was the king's job to tell the citizens what to think about God. A lot of the English people thought otherwise. They were also upset with King James for other reasons. James loved to spend money. The king and his friends had a wonderful time wearing expensive clothing, attending fancy dinners, traveling to exotic places, and playing costly games. William also benefited from this lifestyle. He was brought up to cherish the very best that life could offer. He began his education at a young age and quickly learned the fine arts. Music, art, and theater were pursuits of the wealthy and educated subjects of the monarchy.

Eventually, King James did not have enough money to live such a rich lifestyle. The king had married a woman from Denmark named Anne, who loved beautiful jewels and clothes.

Queen Elizabeth had ruled England before King James and had done a fairly good job of meeting her own royal needs while also trying to meet the needs of her people. James did no such thing. The longer he was in power, the more money and power he gave his friends. He had little regard for the needs of the common people.

Queen Anne's love for jewelry and beautiful clothes added to James I's need for more money, which led to a greater tax burden on the people of England.

Instead of relying on their king, the people found power in the **Parliament.** The Parliament was composed mostly of the educated and the merchant classes of England. English citizens felt that these people better understood their needs.

King James grew tired of listening to the governing voices that opposed his careless handling of the country. If James needed more money, he would make the people pay more taxes. The king had favorite merchants. He ruled that the people could only buy products like soap, wine, or salt from these special businesses.

By the time a teenaged William Berkeley entered Oxford University, King James had handled the troublesome problem of Parliament. He had grown tired of the people's constant objections to the way he ruled, so he dissolved Parliament. The king did not like the voice of the English people, so he silenced it.

William was not affected by all the turmoil his country was experiencing. While England plunged into **economic depression,** the ruling class and its many friends continued to live the high life of feast and favoritism. William took to his studies and spent his young manhood surrounded by the intellectual and creative members of the upper class.

Ætatis suæ 21. Aº.1616.

Matoaks als Rebecka daughter to the mighty Prince Powhatan Emperour of Attanoughkomouck als Virginia converted and baptized in the Christian faith, and Wife to the worll Mr Tho: Rolff.

Pocahontas (pictured above) was married to John Rolfe while he was on his expedition for King James I to the New World. Their marriage brought a short period of peace between English settlers and the native tribes of the area.

A Faraway Alternative

Even while King James was creating many problems in his own country, he supported England's desire to overtake or colonize new worlds beyond the Atlantic Ocean. The king knew that France and Spain were going around the world and taking over new lands as colonies.

Colonizing new land meant that England would have more power in the world. By trading materials found in the new lands, the king would have more money, too. More than anything, James always needed money. He spent much of his time trying to find ways to make more.

The king did not have to use his own money for these colonizing expeditions. A private company would plan and pay for the trip with money invested by those who chose to go on it. All the company needed was a **charter** from the king which granted the right of a company to go forth in a ship or ships to a foreign shore in the name of the king of England.

In the year William was born, a charter was granted to the Virginia Company for three ships to sail abroad. Stories went around the country claiming gold and unlimited land could be found on the other side of the great ocean. The Virginia Company posted signs throughout London, hoping to find enough men upset with the way things were in England and willing to leave the country. They also needed the courage to start a new life in a place they had never been.

In 1606, the three ships set sail with almost 150 men for the foreign shore. It was a harsh and long journey across very dangerous waters. The ships were stocked with grains, weapons,

Bibles, and articles to trade with the native people.

For four months the ships traveled the rough waters in storm and calm, ice and rain. The original excitement the passengers felt upon leaving their mother country quickly dimmed under the stress of ocean travel. The visions of gold and power were replaced by irritable quarreling among the men who had little room to move around the ships during the seemingly endless voyage.

Before leaving England, the Virginia Company had ordered that the captain be in sole command of the voyage. The company knew such adventures could be dangerous and long, and that some chain of command would need to be established. The king also had his say over the establishment of a new England on the distant shores. He had given one man a sealed envelope that held the name of seven of the passengers. These seven men would be the king's choice for a council in the land.

A lot of brave or desperate men had sailed to the New World by the end of the 16th century. Weary sailors who were fortunate enough to return safely to their homeland told wild stories of oceans with islands full of devils who would make howling sounds. They told of huge sea serpents that could swallow ships whole. Some men said they saw creatures, that they called mermaids, having the head and torso of women but the fins of a fish. The mermaids would sing songs so loud and sweet the sailors wanted to come to shore to see them.

Since they did not have much else to do on board, some of the men got into arguments about who was going to be in charge once they got to the new land. But eventually, the ships did arrive. After seeing nothing but the flat horizon of the ocean for so many months, America looked like a paradise to the weary travelers.

The ships arrived in America in the Chesapeake Bay (in what we now know as Virginia). The voyagers had not been on shore for long before they were attacked by some of the native people who lived in the area. The English called them "Indians."

Chesapeake Bay provided convenient shelter for their ships but it could not protect early settlers from the dangers they faced onshore.

The English had not expected such a harsh greeting. They had envisioned exchanging presents and Bibles. The colonists had intended to teach belief in the Christian God to them.

After the first attack, the colonists moved up a long river that they quickly named the James River.

Finding a safe area, the men immediately set about building a church, some thatched huts, and a fort to ward off further attacks. They named their settlement Jamestown. It was very rough going for the hardy group, however. They were hungry and struggled to survive.

By 1608, only half of the original Virginia Company group was alive. Since no women had come on the voyage, the normal cycle of society—that of birth and death—was impossible. Death took its toll, unhampered by the promise of new life.

Each man had been told that he would be given 100 acres of free land for the price of their voyage, but it mattered little to the dying colony. In 1615, more men were recruited from England. It was realized that laborers who could work the land and produce products to sell abroad were needed so that the colonists could make a decent and healthy living. Five hundred more men came to Jamestown, but they still needed a source of income.

The colonists, while loyal to the king, had fled the restrictions of the monarchy. By 1615, an iron discipline ruled the settlers. True to their English heritage, the first thing the settlers did was create a code of laws. However, the settlers actually hated living in such a strict way. One thing the code dictated was that the colonists must not be idle. Colonist John Rolfe took the code to heart and formed a plan.

Tobacco was a substance sought after in many parts of the world. The early Spanish explorers of North and South America found some Indian cultures used the tobacco leaf in religious ceremonies. When the Spaniards used tobacco, they would often soak it in wine or molasses and roll it into balls or thick rolls.

Tobacco had also been smoked by the court of Queen Elizabeth in the 1500s. The English would inhale the substance through pipes. When it first came to Europe, tobacco was used as a medicine. Many people thought anything that smelled really strong had to have some healthful qualities, so it was used to treat many diseases such as bronchitis, asthma, and headaches.

The young king of France, Francis II, is believed to have died because of tobacco. Tobacco was used to make an ointment that was applied to his skin. He probably died from **nicotine** poisoning. The addictive drug nicotine–a chemical that is found in tobacco leaves–is poisonous to the human body in large quantities.

Prior to 1615, the West Indies was virtually the only source of tobacco for the English people. The tobacco grown in the Roanoke area by the Indians was too harsh for the settlers to smoke. The colonists were willing to wait a long time for an import of West Indian tobacco from England which was milder to the smoker.

Then things changed for the English, and for the colonists. John Rolfe married an Indian princess named Pocahontas. She was just 12 years old at the time. The marriage allowed the settlers to have a sort of peace with many of the local tribes.

The new relationship with the natives also provided Rolfe with different kinds of tobacco seeds which he got from the Indians. After some trial and error and a couple of years, Rolfe finally produced a nice crop of tobacco that was pleasing to the settlers' tongues.

The colonists of Jamestown finally had a way to make money. In 1616, the first shipment of tobacco—a total of 2,500 pounds—was ready for export to England; 20,000 pounds were shipped in 1617; and the settlers packed 50,000 pounds of tobacco leaves off to their mother country in 1618.

When King James sent the first three ships off to Virginia with his blessing, he never thought his subjects would end up growing tobacco to survive. In fact, King James hated smoking so much that he actually was the head of a vigorous, antismoking movement in his country.

James was never at a loss for words, and he likened tobacco fumes to the awful smoke of hell itself. He claimed its use was bad for the brain, horrible to the nose, and a danger to a person's lungs.

But like it or not, King James's colonists found their means of survival in the farming and trade of tobacco. More and more laborers arrived in Jamestown from England to work the tobacco fields. Some plantations were as large as 1,000 acres and required a lot of workers to harvest each crop.

Many people who could not afford the cost of the trip to America came as **indentured servants.** They would sign an agreement to work a certain number of years on a **plantation.** At the end of their contract, they would be given land of their own or become tenant farmers.

It was at this time that the first African laborers were brought to America. They were puchased as slaves. The black workers were usually not given an indentured contract. Most of Western Europe

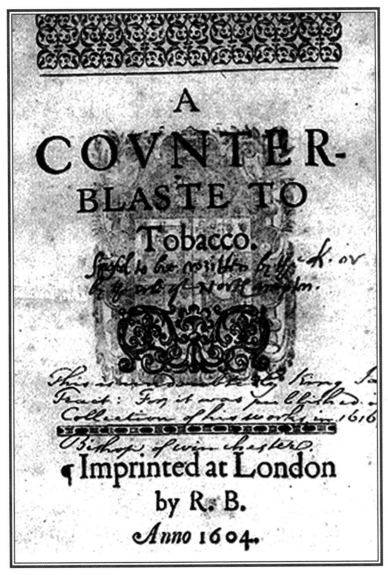

This pamphlet expressed King James's strong dislike for tobacco. It came as quite a shock to him when the first shipments from the Jamestown colony were almost entirely composed of tobacco.

considered people with black skin an inferior sort of people who should not be regarded as free men. It was a belief rooted deeply in ignorance and fear of the unknown.

Native Indians, who had darker skins than the colonists, were regarded at worst as noble savages who had admirable ways but were steeped in strange traditions that needed to be changed by the white man. However, the black people who came from places like Africa were completely denied recognition as full human beings. European mythology considered all things black as bad or evil, and all things white as good and pure.

Only a few Africans came to Virginia in the 17th century to become slaves of the white plantation owners, but it was the beginning of a long history of **prejudice**, that would extend into the 20th century.

John Rolfe's experiment had been a success and shortly after the first shipment arrived in England, he took his young bride, Pocahontas, and their son, Thomas, to England. A group of young Indians went with the Rolfe family so they could be educated there. Before Pocahontas could return to her native Virginia, she caught a disease and died.

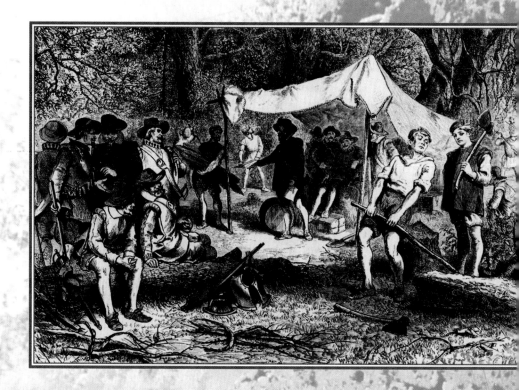

The Jamestown settlement began to grow
in both size and importance. Soon, coun-
cils were organized to govern the colony,
families arrived, and new industries were
welcomed to the New World. Yet, even in
times of prosperity, the Jamestown settlement was never far from danger and new
threats to the growing community seemed
to appear around every corner.

3

A Governed Life and Deadly Strife

Jamestown became the center of the rapidly growing Virginia colony. By the year 1619, the colonists had begun to feel stronger and attempted to organize a system of laws to govern the growing population. An aristocrat named Lord Delaware had loosely held everything together through instructions of the king's court until his death in 1618.

Sir George Yeardley was named governor in 1619. He was helped by a group of six men called the Council of State. Two men from each plantation had been elected to represent the people. This meeting of the Council of State and representatives who were called **burgesses** gave the new Virginians a representative democracy. This form of government was the foundation for the government in the United States today.

Since Virginia was a royal colony, everything the House of Burgesses did was written down and then sent off to England for the king's approval. However, the government body went on with its work as it waited for the king's reply. That reply often took weeks to arrive.

The colony and its new government were still under the control of the company that had first brought the colonists to shore. The assembled representatives had the job of making the colonists pay taxes to pay for the church. They also ruled on matters of public behavior, trade with other countries, and the price at which to sell tobacco.

Women who came to Virginia to get married stayed with certain families until they found a husband. When a man took a bride, he paid 120 pounds of tobacco for the price of her trip.

Special racks and sheds were built to cure the tobacco to prevent it from spoiling during shipping to England.

In the beginning, tobacco was the main crop grown in Virginia. But company owners soon realized it was not a good idea to have a whole society rely on only one crop as a means of survival. The Assembly ordered that each plantation cultivate a number of wild grapevines so that wine could be made and sold. They also ordered the planting and harvesting of flax plants

Tobacco was very easy to grow. When the plants were young, workers pulled up weeds that might choke off the new plants. But after the leaves began to sprout, little labor was necessary.

The leaves were picked while they were green. When the colonists harvested their first crops, they piled the leaves in large bundles and let them dry in the sun. Then the tobacco was shipped to England. Soon it was discovered this method caused the leaves to rot. A way of hanging the leaves outside on racks was devised. Once dried, the leaves were brought into houses specially made just to cure the tobacco. This proved a safe way of supplying a good and sellable crop.

to make linen and the planting of mulberry trees to provide a habitat for the silkworm, from whose cocoons silk is made.

A colonist named Captain Newport had ventured many miles up the James River and found large deposits of iron ore in the ground. In a short time, an iron foundry was built at that site. English miners came to Virginia to mine the ore that was then **smelted** on the spot into pig iron, the most basic and crude form of iron.

Jamestown and its surrounding towns seemed blessed with success. Its many undertakings provided colonists with an increasingly better standard of living. The settlers were getting along very well with the native Indians. The local Powhatan Confederation of Indians was promising an undying friendship with the colonists.

By 1618, the leadership of the Confederation had been taken over by Opechancanough, an Indian chieftain whose early experience with invaders had been deadly. Opechancanough had lived in the southwestern part of America when the Spaniards landed and brutally fought and defeated the Indians. After that defeat, the chief fled east, fighting his way through tribes and various settlements until he came to Virginia.

He and his tribes were living in the area along the James River on which the iron foundry was built. About 20 miles below the foundry, a school had been built for the purpose of educating both white and Indian children in Christian ways. George Thorpe, an adviser to the king, had been sent to Virginia to head the new school. He was a well-known scholar and devout Christian.

When George Thorpe met Chief Opechancanough, Thorpe believed everything the chief told him. The chief suggested that the colonial children could visit the Indian reservations to learn Indian ways just as the Indian children were to visit the colonial villages. Thorpe thought the chief was so honest that the Englishman built a house for the chief to stay in. But the whole time, the chief was setting up Thorpe and all the colonists for a major act of revenge. The chief had never lost his hatred for the white man. He planned a giant attack to be carried out at many locations at exactly the same time: eight o'clock in the morning on March 22, 1622. It was the Christian Good Friday.

More than 80 locations were hit at that time by a fierce and deadly onslaught of Indians. By the end of the attacks, more than a quarter of the colony's population had been brutally killed. Many more would have died in Jamestown if a young Indian boy named Chanco had not told a settler what was happening. Chanco had been ordered by his Indian relatives to kill the white godfather he was living with. The boy could not do it. Instead, Chanco told his godfather, who immediately rowed his boat to Jamestown to warn the people. By the time the Indians arrived on their deadly mission, many settlers had armed themselves so they could successfully fight back their enemy.

The eight-year period of peace and prosperity of the colony of Jamestown had ended in a horrible fashion. News of the terrible massacre was brought to the royal court and eventually to the ears of the students of Oxford University. Little did young William Berkeley realize that his future would be plagued by that very problem in the colony when he became governor of Virginia.

William Berkeley graduated from Oxford in 1623. Almost immediately following his graduation, he fell into favor with the king and became a prominent adviser. William's talents and ability to remain in good standing with Charles I served him well.

4

Sir William Sets Virginia's Course

The **massacre** in Virginia devastated the people of the colony both physically and emotionally. King James used this incident to get rid of the Virginia Company, which had basically governed the colony since its beginning. James had always thought that the company did not pay enough attention to what he wanted in Virginia. The king revoked the charter of the Virginia Company in 1624.

Virginia was now considered a royal province. The king would pick its governors and its council from now on.

When Charles I came to the throne in 1625, he did not know anyone besides his family and the people in the king's court. He was only 24 years old, but throughout his young life he had written a notebook full of sayings, most of which he had heard from his father. These sayings helped Charles learn how to conduct himself as king. Because he did not know very much about ordering the citizens of England, they did not think he was a good king.

William Berkeley had graduated from Queen's College in Oxford on February 14, 1623. On July 10, 1629, he received a master of arts degree from St. Edmund Hall, Oxford. William then became one of the king's personal advisers. He was aware of what happened at the king's court.

King James died a year after he took away the Virginia Company's charter. He was succeeded by Charles I. William was a friend to the new king. Charles was not considered a very effective king. He did not have the strength of character to act on the things he said he believed. He cared more about arts and less about battle. Charles was fond of painters and had a good eye for the best artists of his era.

Like the king, William was also interested in the arts. He especially loved the theater. William wrote one successful play, *The Lost Lady,* which was called a tragic comedy. No one knows what other plays William wrote, but he was considered to be a good playwright during his time.

A bright, ambitious man, William was appointed commissioner of colonial Canadian affairs by the king. He worked in that position from an office in London. After the publication of William's play in 1639, Charles I made William a knight of the royal court. The talented man was now known as Sir William Berkeley.

Little did he know it then, but William's future was to be more successful than the king's. Charles sent William to Virginia to be the colony's governor in 1642. William was the colony's last royal governor.

The first year of his term marked the first year of a civil war in England. Charles I became so unpopular with both his Parliament (which had been reestablished under James's reign) and countrymen that war broke out. It was the one and only war that pitted Englishmen against one another. Matters of religious freedom and the economy set brother against brother, father against son.

While his mother country suffered the torments of war, William urged many of his fellow countrymen to come and live in his new home of Virginia. William worked hard to help the English government understand the special, independent needs of his colony.

William was in his mid-30s when he came to Virginia and quickly established himself as a popular leader. He tried to fulfill the needs of both the rich and the poor. He encouraged his people to explore the lands beyond Virginia. The colonists were very happy with the new governor when he stopped making them pay a poll tax.

Burgesses representing the people in the General Assembly were encouraged to speak freely of their concerns. William's governorship saw the introduction of coins as a means of

Charles I, shown here with his wife Henrietta Maria, was never respected by his subjects because of his inability to establish his power as king. His fondness for the arts and the theater far outweighed his abilities as a military commander or as a leader of his people.

paying for goods. The settlers no longer paid debts with tobacco.

There were, however, certain things that William did not allow. He would not let Puritans

In Virginia, as in England, people were addressed according to their station in life. Cavaliers, gentlemen of wealth who supported the king, were called "Mister." Those of little or no educa-tion and spare means were called by their last names or by the type of work they did, like carpenter, landlord, or miller.

or Quakers practice their religion openly. As tolerant as he was in other areas, William simply could not stop persecuting the two **sects.**

William had enjoyed the highest educational advan-tage in England and yet, when he arrived in Vir-ginia, he showed little inter-est in promoting learning among his people. He would not sponsor the building of any free school. William also pub-licly stated he was happy that no printing press existed in the area.

Despite these shortcomings, life in Virginia went smoothly for a while. The average farmer lived fairly comfortably in a brick house with a shingled roof and a large brick chimney at one end. Richer colonists had similarly made homes which were larger, and usually two stories. The houses were generally surrounded by vegetable and flower gardens. Nearby, smaller structures would be used for smoking and curing hams. Small buildings also housed blacksmith tools.

William built himself a huge brick dwelling near Jamestown proper at a place he called Green Spring. He encouraged others to build their own brick houses. William was comfortably settled into this new world and did not miss the much different, more hectic pace of London and the court.

William lived the life of a gentleman in his spacious plantation. In his spare time, he conducted agricultural experiments. William encouraged his people to grow crops other than tobacco. He grew cotton, flax, and rice on his land. William used this cotton and flax to weave his own fabric and encouraged his citizens to also be self-reliant. He remained a staunch Royalist, but he always seemed to work toward the best interests of all the community over which he ruled.

Peace was shattered in 1644 when Chief Opechancanough made one last attempt to kill off the hated white settlers who had invaded his land. His assault lasted for two years. William was so successful organizing his people against the determined enemy that the Indians finally asked for a peace treaty. The treaty was drawn up in 1646, and the peace lasted for the next 30 years.

Across the sea, Charles I was not doing well at all. By 1647, it was clear he was on the losing side against his people and his Parliament. Parliament held Charles captive and demanded he meet certain demands. Parliament wanted an election every two years. They wanted to take control of the army from the king and insisted that all **Protestants** be allowed to practice their religion in England.

Charles I was a stubborn man and refused to give in to Parliament's demands. More fighting followed, and in the end, the king was brought before a Court of High Justice. A rebellious leader named Oliver Cromwell insisted the king be tried for treason for waging war against Parliament.

Charles was found guilty and sentenced to death. January 30, 1649, was a cold and wintry day outside of Whitehall Palace, the king's official residence. As if in mockery, a **scaffold** was built in front of the palace. Charles I was escorted slowly toward the executioner's block. The English, who usually enjoyed such spectacles with a great amount of cheering and enthusiasm, stood silent as this dark moment of history was acted out. They knew their king had failed them in many ways. They also knew he was paying the ultimate price for his failures. In a moment, the executioner's axe fell down heavily and, with that swift chop, ended both Charles's reign and his life.

Oliver Cromwell assumed a form of civilian leadership of England. Religious freedom became a reality. The economy of the country also improved.

William, who had remained faithful to his king, left his governorship during the period of Cromwell's rule. Cromwell had sent ships full of men to take over Virginia's royal council. William had gotten an army together to fend them off, but in the end, he decided it would be in his best interests to stay at Green Spring during this fateful time.

However, Virginia did not suffer. The colony actually achieved greater democracy and economic success. Left to themselves, the colonists fared very well.

Ten years later, in 1658, Oliver Cromwell died. The local burgesses immediately thought that a Stuart king would assume the throne. Although little was known about William's pursuits during this time, the colonists of Virginia remembered him well. They went out to Green Spring to talk with their former governor. William was asked to return as governor of Virginia. William said that he would, but only if a Stuart king took the throne.

Charles II, a member of the Stuart family, did assume the throne after the death of Oliver Cromwell. England was in a financial mess when the king arrived. But the last 20 years of fighting and protesting against the economic and religious wrongs in England had brought the people a greater sense of independence from an inflexible royal rule.

Charles II's reign marked the beginning of the Restoration. Parliament had more freedom to rule in the name of its citizens. People were no longer persecuted for their religious beliefs. This allowed greater freedom of thought and creativity.

When William once again became governor of his beloved colony, Virginia was different. The population had grown to 40,000 citizens, and English families of great stature had arrived to begin new lives. Just as the colony had changed, so too had William.

He immediately got rid of the democratic policies under which the colonists had flourished

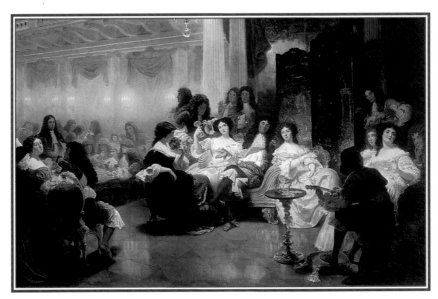

When Charles II became king after Cromwell's death, he restored the practice of many activities like dancing, acting, and card playing that had been forbidden by the Puritans. Charles, like his father and grandfather, enjoyed having lavish parties with his courtiers at his palace at Whitehall.

in the 1650s. He put in his own Parliament, which did whatever he wanted. There had been a system of independent courts set in place to take care of local matters. William gathered them into his own power, taking away the rights of the people. He had his own favorite people, but he showed little care for the average settler's needs.

William gave his friends generous gifts and made sure that they did not have to pay some of the taxes he made the poorer people pay. William would not let an election be held for seats in the House of Burgesses. However, the colonists had become too independent during the upheaval in England to want to put up with William's strict rule.

William did support the rights of Virginians when Charles II came to power and enacted the Navigation Acts. Charles wanted to have a very strong navy and a good merchant marine so that money could come to the kingdom from the sale of goods. He thought the best way to make sure this happened was to make a law that the colonists could not sell their tobacco to any other country except England. Charles said they could not buy or sell a lot of other things from other countries. Everyone was forced to obey these Navigation Acts.

During the period known as the Restoration, Charles II promoted the pursuit of science. He was not a particularly bright man, but he would converse with the most famous scientists of the time: Robert Boyle, the physicist; Robert Hooke, the inventor; Edmond Halley, the astronomer who discovered the famous comet, and the great mathematician and physicist Isaac Newton.

Charles II also decided to wage a war with the Dutch who bought a lot of tobacco from America. This made the colonists mad. They had been used to selling their tobacco to whoever wanted to pay the highest price.

Even William knew this was a bad thing, especially for the average farmer. He protested against the act, although he was putting new taxes on his people at the same time. The colonists were upset with both the king and William. They realized that having the governor back was not such a good idea after all. Rumbles of dissatisfaction ran through the farms and fields along the James River.

William sensed their dissatisfaction and worried about his own future. "How miserable that man is that Governes a People wher six parts of seaven at least are Poore Endebted Discontented and Armed," William wrote about the state of his colony. He knew something was about to happen. Rebellion was brewing.

The Jamestown colony survived many hardships during its early years. Under the direction of William Berkeley, it was very successful in the New World. But rebellion, led by young Nathaniel Bacon, soon gripped the colony.

Bacon's Rebellion

Young Nathaniel Bacon could hear the excited crowd of men yelling for him from the distant shore. The men shouted his name, "Bacon! Bacon!" repeatedly as Bacon crossed the James River in a boat with two companions.

The 28-year-old plantation owner was not just crossing a river on a spring day in 1676. He was embarking on a short and wild adventure that would go down in history. As a young member of the privileged upper class, Nathaniel had learned firsthand some lessons about citizenship. Nathaniel's father Thomas and his grandfather were key figures in the vigorous protests staged against Charles I. The Bacon father-and-son duo led many demonstrations that accused the tyrannical king of undermining basic laws of British government. Nathaniel felt a the pride of his birthright within him as he looked across the water.

The men gathered on the riverbank were a diverse group of settlers. Some, like Bacon, had come from wealth and status from the mother country, England. Upon his arrival in Virginia, Bacon had been given a large grant of land and a seat on the governing council in 1675. William Berkeley's wife was related to Nathaniel Bacon by marriage. William might have been known as a crotchety old man during his second term as governor, but he welcomed the young man into the powerful and elite Jamestown society.

Other men waiting on the river's edge for Nathaniel Bacon were members of the lower classes. They were angry and committed to a cause. Their mission was to kill as many Indians as they could.

Sir Nathaniel Bacon.
From the Original, Painted by himself, at Gorhambury.

Nathaniel Bacon's desire for a commission to attack any and all Native Americans he encountered was the beginning of his long-running dispute with William Berkeley.

Nathaniel Bacon was a brooding young man. His father had sent Nathaniel and his wife with some money to Virginia in order that he become a responsible adult. As his father's only son and cousin to the famous Sir Francis Bacon, Nathaniel had big shoes to fill.

Nathaniel had known little of the new American colony of Jamestown. He did not know it had been plagued by many hardships: famine, storms, territorial fights with Indians, and increasingly heavy taxation levied both locally and from abroad.

By the time Nathaniel arrived in Virginia, many colonists had become frustrated by the way William Berkeley was handling the local Indians. He considered some Indian tribes a threat, but he courted most of them in order to reap the benefits of trading furs such as the skins of beaver to make into hats and other articles of clothing.

Consequently, he offered little help to the local settlers when they started running into trouble with various tribes. Skirmishes with some local tribes often resulted in many deaths on both sides.

In the summer of 1675, members of the Doeg Indian tribe attacked the plantation of a man named Thomas Mathews. They were upset that Mathews had conducted some business with the tribe but had not paid the Doegs what they were due. The raid resulted in several of the Doegs being killed. Rumors about the incident spread throughout the area and caused tempers to flare.

Before long, a band of **vigilante** colonists struck back at the Indians. Unfortunately, they did not attack the Doegs. By mistake, the colonists attacked the Susquehanaugs, a tribe that had been friendly with the settlers. **Mayhem** resulted, and more Indian attacks occurred. The colonists urged William to launch an investigation immediately. However, a meeting he arranged with several Indian chiefs ended in the murder of the chiefs.

Because of continued attacks, bands of irate colonists wanted action, and they wanted it right away. The Doeg incident was the last straw in a bale of complaints a lot of colonists had against the hardships they faced in their daily lives in Virginia.

Nathaniel did not intend to get in the middle of any trouble, but he did want to make the Indian problem go away. Nathaniel yelled his thoughts to a group of protestors at one point, "If the Redskins meddle with me, I will harry them, commission or no commission." A **commission** was permission from the governor to allow colonists to fight legally against an enemy. No colonist was given a commission by William.

In July 1676, on the shores of the James River, Nathaniel Bacon agreed to lead the mob of protestors. The first thing they planned to do was meet with the governor. Bacon told William he would finance his own expedition against the troublesome Indian tribes. But William refused to give Bacon permission to do this.

No matter how Nathaniel pleaded his case, William would not give Bacon the commission to allow him to lead his men as an army against the Indians. Nathaniel's band went into the woods anyway, and arranged with the

By the time Nathaniel Bacon arrived in Virginia, many colonists in the Jamestown settlement and nearby areas had become frustrated by the way William Berkeley was handling the local Indians. They took matters into their own hands, attacking the Indians without William's permission.

Occaneechee Indians to join forces in an attack against the Susquehanaugs. After the first tribe was killed, Nathaniel's men started quarrelling with the Occaneechees. Nathaniel's men then completely destroyed the Occaneechee village, along with most of its people.

William was extremely upset by the killing and publicly declared Nathaniel Bacon a traitor and a rebel. Because William had not commissioned Bacon to lead men in any armed conflict, Bacon could be found guilty of **treason**–the worst crime a citizen can commit against his country. This behavior was punishable by death.

Nathaniel did return to Jamestown after the Occaneechee incident, but for a time, William's **militia** of 300 men had tried to capture him on the run.

In Jamestown, Nathaniel appeared before the governor with 50 armed men as protection. William, now 70, was not so hard-hearted as he sometimes appeared to be. He pardoned his relative instead of issuing a writ of execution.

During the chaos of Bacon's Rebellion, many innocent Native American settlements, like this re-creation at Jamestown, were destroyed by Bacon and his men.

Nathaniel, either through force of personality, persuasion, or power, was reinstated into the capital's governing council. Nathaniel left with his earnest soldiers and returned to the woods to fight any Indians they could find. Nathaniel was now a man with a purpose and 500 men to help achieve it. He and his men returned to Jamestown and forced William to give him the commission to legally lead his men against the enemy.

Once Nathaniel received the commission, he demanded that his followers swear allegiance to him completely. Nathaniel set about a stronger campaign against the Indians, plundering their villages and stealing the furs that had been prepared for trade. Nathaniel even attacked the friendly Pamunkey Indian tribe.

Nathaniel soon received word that almost as quickly as he had been given his commission, William declared it invalid. William had had enough fighting. Taking a small group of followers with him, William fled Jamestown to the eastern shores of Virginia for a short time.

After killing off all the Pamunkeys, Nathaniel returned once again to Jamestown and laid siege to the city. William had returned from his retreat, but after a week's siege by Nathaniel, the governor and his followers once again ran away in the middle of the night.

After wreaking so much **havoc,** Nathaniel had no interest in making peace with the governor. Matters had gotten so far out of hand that he claimed to have no faith in any pact the governor would attempt to make. Both William and Nathaniel had tried to amass support by promising slaves and indentured servants freedom if they joined their forces. Nathaniel had been more successful at recruiting than William.

Nathaniel's popularity had grown throughout the countryside. He succeeded because he had the ability to control his men. Nathaniel was very careful to make sure that his followers did what he said and no more. He would not allow them to take things that did not belong to them.

They were not allowed to destroy things just because they were angry.

He had specific reasons for doing what he did. Nathaniel did not want his carefully thought-out protests to be seen as the acts of a crazy mob. He cared about his own rights and the rights of his fellow colonists.

Nathaniel brought his followers together in one meeting and locked the doors. He insisted that everyone present sign an oath of loyalty to him and against the governor. Many of the men were afraid to go that far. But the doors were locked. Since they had come of their own free will, they had little choice but to sign the oath and follow their new leader, no matter what the consequeneces proved to be.

When Nathaniel and his 600 men marched on the State House, where William was meeting with the burgesses, the old man and the young man stood face-to-face, yet they remained oceans apart in their beliefs.

In exasperation, William tore open his shirt

and shouted to Nathaniel, "Here! Shoot me— 'fore God, fair mark. Shoot!"

Nathaniel had no interest in killing the old man, but William just wanted to end it all. He drew a sword and challenged Nathaniel to a duel.

"Sir," Nathaniel told William, "I came not, nor intend, to hurt a hair on your Honor's head. And as for your sword, your Honor may please to put it up; it shall rust in its scabbard before ever I shall desire you to draw it. I come for a commission against the heathen who daily inhumanly murder us and spill our brethren's blood. And a commission I will have before I go!"

Nathaniel just wanted the commission. But to put a little extra scare into old William, he ordered his men, "Prime your guns!"

By now, Nathaniel and his men believed they were leading a righteous cause. Nathaniel decided to destroy all traces of the old aristocratic governor's life in Jamestown. Nathaniel would not shoot William in cold blood, but he did order his men to set fire to 1,500,000 pounds of tobacco. The impassioned men even moved as one to destroy their own Jamestown houses.

Filled with a sense of power, Nathaniel Bacon had only been in the New World for two years when, in September 1676, he and his men burned down the entire city of Jamestown. It was his reasoning that if William returned to the capital, he would have nothing to recapture.

After the fire, Nathaniel instituted a new General Assembly, called Bacon's Assembly. Its purpose was to enact laws that would reduce the privileges that had been automatically granted to a specific wealthy minority. The legislation attempted to give the common people a greater chance to succeed and have a voice in the new government. Additional laws were enacted to deal with Indian affairs, settlement along the James River, and regulation of the army.

And then, just as fate had brought Nathaniel Bacon quickly into a strange, dynamic, and dangerous position of power, it just as speedily struck him down with death. He became ill and died in a matter of days. Without its leader, the rebellion also ended.

Within a month of the burning of Jamestown, Nathaniel was secretly buried. His followers returned home to resume their lives, except for the 23 who William had hanged as traitors.

Sir WILLIAM BERKELEY *Brother to JOHN the first Lord BERKELEY of STRATTON.*

The aftermath of Bacon's Rebellion left a permanent scar on William's character, and the king became impatient with the stubborn governor's attempts to seek revenge for the uprising.

A Fall from Grace

While some disagreed with Nathaniel Bacon and his rebellion, others saw him as a courageous hero who virtually began the colonial trek toward freedom from England 100 years later.

Before the fateful rebellion against William Berkeley, Nathaniel had written to a friend in England: "Finding that the country was basely, for a small, sordid gain, betrayed, and the lives of the poor inhabitants wretchedly sacrificed, I resolved to stand in this ruinous gap, risking my life and fortune to all hazards."

But Nathaniel's tempestuous display of leadership was his birthright. Like William, Nathaniel was born into the luxurious elegance of the English aristocracy in the middle of the 17th century. It was a strange twist of fate that two Englishmen bred from a similar, comfortable upbringing should travel such different philosophical roads only to meet, as enemies, at an intersection of history, thousands of miles from the place of their birth.

As the year 1677 began, William Berkeley's Virginia was trying to recover from the disastrous rebellion. He had satisfied his sense of revenge by killing as many rebels as he could. But rubbing out the last traces of Nathaniel's wild spree could not erase the humiliation the governor had felt at the hands of the young Englishman.

William made sure the widows and children of known rebels suffered for their husbands' and fathers' deeds. He went so far to feed his anger that Charles II got disgusted with him. "That old fool has hanged more men in that naked country than I have done for the murder of my father!" the king is said to have uttered.

When William came to the new land to become governor, he could never have imagined what lay ahead. He was quite a fortunate man. For the most part, many colonists barely survived a few months or years in America before dying from disease or Indian attack. William lived the life of luxury and honor, reaping the benefits of providence and the hardiness and faithfulness of his people.

Charles II grew increasingly disgusted with William's desire to take revenge against those who had joined in Bacon's Rebellion and, as a result, removed William as governor of the colony.

However, William grew careless in the end, and that lack of care brought with it his downfall. Charles II sent word to Virginia that

William was to be removed from the office of governor.

For a number of months, the king's messengers were unable to get the stubborn old man to leave Jamestown. Finally, William was worn down, and he did leave, setting sail for England.

William thought he would be able to see the king and try to regain the royal favor. But it was not to be. The long sea journey and his age caught up with him, and he had to take to his bed when he reached the shores of England. Before the year was out and before he could see the king, William died on June 9, 1677.

GLOSSARY

burgess a representative in the house of lawmaking in colonial Virginia and Maryland

charter a grant of land, rights, privileges or franchises given by the ruler of a state or country

commission authority granted by the governer of a colony

economic depression a period marked by a slowdown in business activity, underemployment, and falling prices and wages

havoc general destruction

indentured servant a person who is under a contract binding him to work for another

massacre the merciless killing of many people

mayhem a state of disorder

militia an army composed of private citizens in time of emergency

nicotine a toxic and addictive substance contained in tobacco

Parliament the national lawmaking body of Great Britain

plantation a large farm set on an area of land used for growing cultivated crops

prejudice a judgment or opinion formed without basis in fact

Protestant a member of a Christian denomination that denied the authority of the Catholic Church

scaffold a raised platform on which criminals are executed

sect a religious group that breaks off from a larger group

smelt to melt down iron ore and change into pig iron, the most basic form of iron

treason betrayal of one's country

vigilante a group of people without legal rights who take the law into their own hands

CHRONOLOGY

1606 William Berkeley is born in Bruton, England, the son of Maurice Berkeley.

1624 Receives bachelor of arts degree from Queen's College at Oxford.

1629 Receives a master of arts degree; becomes popular with the king and a member of the king's council.

1632 Appointed English commissioner for colonial Canada; holds office in England.

1639 Publishes a play, *The Lost Lady;* knighted by Charles I in July.

1642 Appointed governor of Virginia by King Charles.

1649 Charles I beheaded in England for the crime of treason.

1652 Oliver Cromwell comes into power; William flees to Green Spring, Virginia, relinquishing his governor's seat.

1660 Virginia Assembly chooses William to return as governor; Charles II takes the throne as king of England.

1676 Nathaniel Bacon leads a rebellion, burning the entire city of Jamestown; the uprising ends in Bacon's death and William's reprisals.

1677 Charles II removes William from office of governor; William leaves Virginia in May to return to England; he takes to his bed ill, and dies on June 9.

COLONIAL TIME LINE

1607 Jamestown, Virginia, is settled by the English.

1620 Pilgrims on the *Mayflower* land at Plymouth, Massachusetts.

1623 The Dutch settle New Netherlands, the colony that later becomes New York.

1630 Massachusetts Bay Colony is started.

1634 Maryland is settled as a Roman Catholic colony. Later Maryland becomes a safe place for people with different religious beliefs.

1636 Roger Williams is thrown out of the Massachusetts Bay Colony. He settles Rhode Island, the first colony to give people freedom of religion.

1682 William Penn forms the colony of Pennsylvania.

1688 Pennsylvania Quakers make the first formal protest against slavery.

1692 Trials for witchcraft are held in Salem, Massachusetts.

1712 Slaves revolt in New York. Twenty-one blacks are killed as punishment.

1720 Major smallpox outbreak occurs in Boston. Cotton Mather and some doctors try a new treatment. Many people think the new treatment shouldn't be used.

1754 French and Indian War begins. It ends nine years later.

1761 Benjamin Banneker builds a wooden clock that keeps precise time.

1765 Britain passes the Stamp Act. Violent protests break out in the colonies. The Stamp Act is ended the next year.

1775 The battles of Lexington and Concord begin the American Revolution.

1776 Declaration of Independence is signed.

FURTHER READING

Campbell, Elizabeth A. *Jamestown: The Beginning*. Boston: Little Brown, 1974.

Davis, Burke. *Getting To Know Jamestown*. New York: Coward, McCann & Geoghegan, 1971.

Gill, Harold B., and Ann Finlayson, *Virginia*. Nashville: Thomas Nelson, 1973.

Neal, Harry. *The Virginia Colony*. New York: Edward Hawthorn Books, 1969.

Palmer, Alan. *Kings and Queens of England*. Hong Kong: Mandarin Publishers, 1976.

INDEX

PICTURE CREDITS

ABOUT THE AUTHOR

PHELAN POWELL has been a daily correspondent for the *Michigan City News-Dispatch* and has worked in the Public Affairs Office of the U.S. Coast Guard Reserve. The author of seven Chelsea House books, including one on Tom Cruise and another on John LeClair, Phelan is currently working on other books for various publishers.

Senior Consulting Editor **ARTHUR M. SCHLESINGER, JR.** is the leading American historian of our time. He won the Pulitzer Prize for his book *The Age of Jackson* (1945) and again for *A Thousand Days* (1965). This chronicle of the Kennedy Administration also won a National Book Award. He has written many other books including a multi-volume series, *The Age of Roosevelt*. Professor Schlesinger is the Albert Schweitzer Professor of the Humanities at the City University of New York, and has been involved in several other Chelsea House projects, including the REVOLUTIONARY WAR LEADERS biographies on the most prominent figures of early American history.